THE STORY OF
THE BIBLE

VOLUME II
THE NEW TESTAMENT

Activity Book

Cataloging-in-Publication data on file with the Library of Congress.

Illustrations by Chris Pelicano, Caroline Kiser, and askib/shutterstock.

ISBN: 978-1-61890-716-5

Printed and bound in the United States of America

THE STORY OF
THE BIBLE

VOLUME II
THE NEW TESTAMENT

Activity Book

TAN

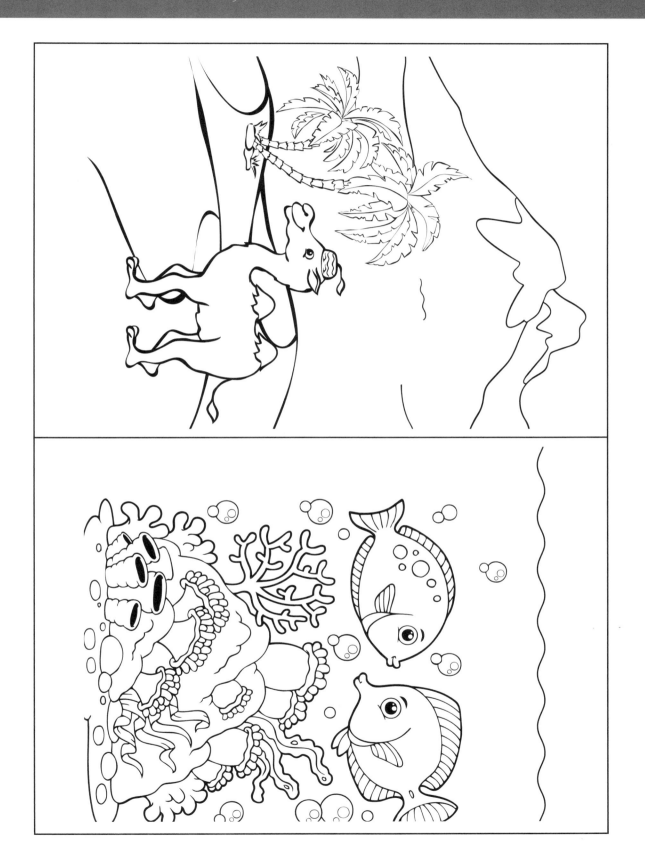

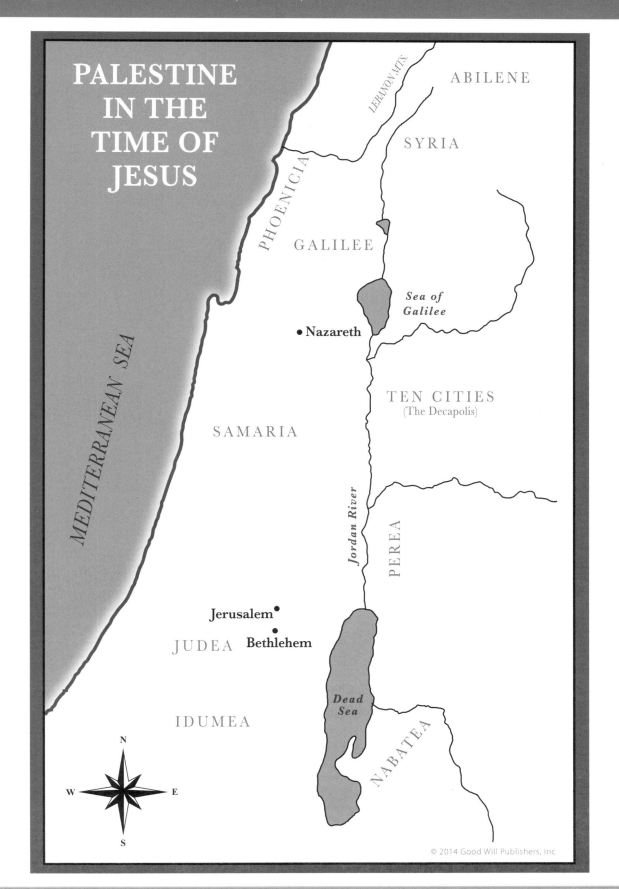

PALESTINE
IN THE
TIME OF
JESUS

LEBANON MTS.

ABILENE

SYRIA

PHOENICIA

GALILEE

Sea of
Galilee

• Nazareth

MEDITERRANEAN SEA

TEN CITIES
(The Decapolis)

SAMARIA

Jordan River

PEREA

Jerusalem •
•
JUDEA   Bethlehem

Dead
Sea

IDUMEA

NABATEA

N
W   E
S

© 2014 Good Will Publishers, Inc

The Birth of Jesus Word Search Clues

1. In what city as Jesus born? _____
2. _____ was the name of Mary's cousin.
3. The angel _____ appeared to Mary.
4. Who was Mary's husband? _____
5. What was the name of the child born to Elizabeth and Zechariah? _____
6. Who was born in a stable in Bethlehem? _____
7. The place where Mary and Joseph lived before they traveled to Bethlehem. _____
8. The father of John the Baptist and husband of Elizabeth. _____
9. "They will call his name _____, which means 'God is with us.'"
10. Also called the magi. _____
11. What is the name of the Mother of God? _____
12. A group of _____ were keeping watch over their flock when an angel of the Lord appeared to them.

The Birth of Jesus Word Search

```
L  Y  W  S  H  E  P  H  E  R  D  S
L  E  I  R  B  A  G  A  S  I  E  W
V  V  D  J  O  H  N  I  R  O  H  C
N  H  E  V  E  L  H  R  O  H  D  M
N  E  T  Q  J  O  B  A  Q  P  N  E
X  A  M  E  H  E  L  H  T  E  B  M
M  X  Z  E  B  T  F  C  Y  S  S  M
A  A  X  A  S  A  O  E  W  O  U  A
E  N  R  U  R  I  Z  Z  C  J  S  N
K  S  S  Y  Z  E  W  I  E  I  K  U
O  E  N  G  B  S  T  B  L  U  A  E
J  H  B  W  W  T  W  H  Y  E  Q  L
```

If you have trouble figuring out the words from your clues, see if you can find the words from this list: Bethlehem, Elizabeth, Emmanuel, Gabriel, Jesus, John, Joseph, Mary, Nazareth, Shepherds, Wisemen, Zechariah.

START

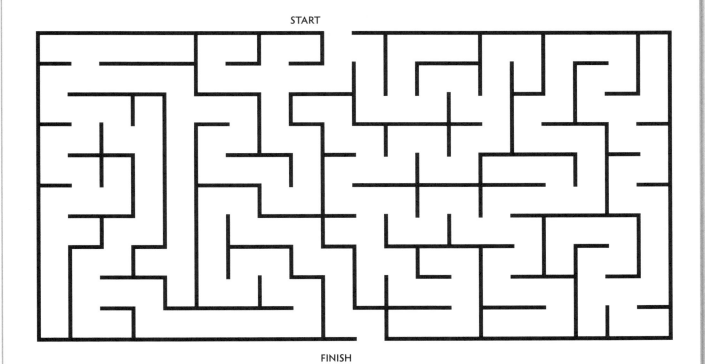

FINISH

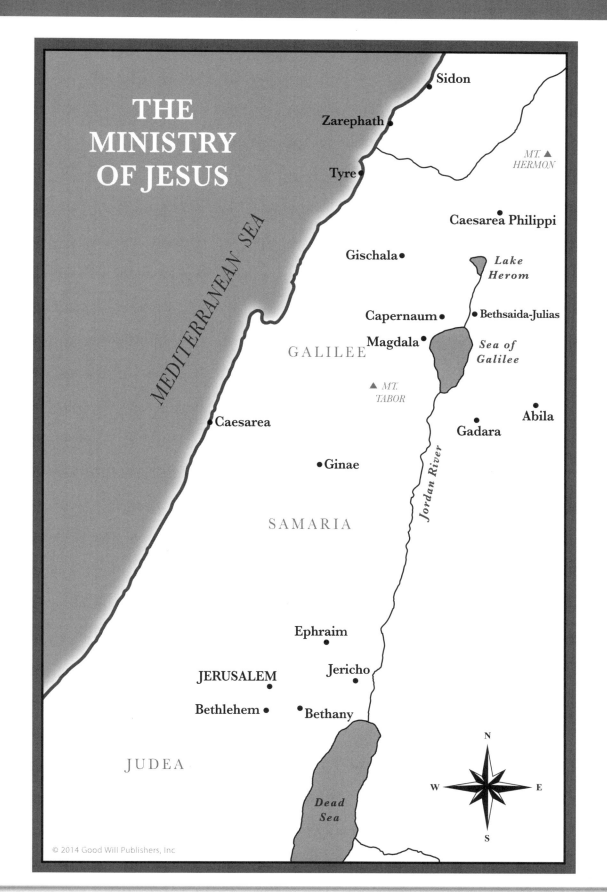

THE
MINISTRY
OF JESUS

MEDITERRANEAN SEA

Sidon

Zarephath

MT. ▲
HERMON

Tyre

Caesarea Philippi

Gischala•

*Lake
Herom*

Capernaum• •Bethsaida-Julias

Magdala•

*Sea of
Galilee*

GALILEE

▲ *MT.
TABOR*

Abila

Gadara

•Caesarea

•Ginae

Jordan River

SAMARIA

Ephraim

Jericho

JERUSALEM

Bethlehem • •Bethany

N

W   E

S

JUDEA

*Dead
Sea*

The Apostles of Jesus Word Search Clues

1. A tax collector. _____
2. Older brother of John and son of Zebedee. _____
3. His name means "the twin." _____
4. Younger brother of James and son of Zebedee. _____
5. The brother of Simon Peter. _____
6. Was known first as Simon, the fisherman. _____
7. Friend of Nathaniel (Bartholomew). _____
8. Son of Alphaeus. _____
9. Betrayed Jesus. _____
10. Called the Zealot. _____
11. Also called Nathaniel. _____
12. Also called Jude. _____

The Apostles of Jesus Word Search

```
N  W  W  Z  T  K  D  P  O  G  B  C
S  U  E  D  D  A  H  T  S  A  O  P
M  W  R  H  D  I  G  T  R  I  I  J
Q  W  D  H  T  W  J  T  T  L  R  U
A  O  N  J  A  T  H  A  I  J  J  D
P  N  A  Q  X  O  A  H  M  Y  N  A
Y  S  H  G  L  L  P  M  B  E  G  S
J  A  O  O  P  D  N  O  M  I  S  T
B  A  M  E  J  K  O  F  F  Z  G  B
G  E  T  L  O  M  S  E  M  A  J  Y
W  E  E  U  K  T  H  O  M  A  S  U
R  R  G  I  I  Q  Z  L  G  D  X  S
```

If you have trouble figuring out the words from your clues, see if you can find the words from this list: Andrew, Bartholomew, James, John, Judas, James, Matthew, Peter, Philip, Simon, Thaddeus, Thomas

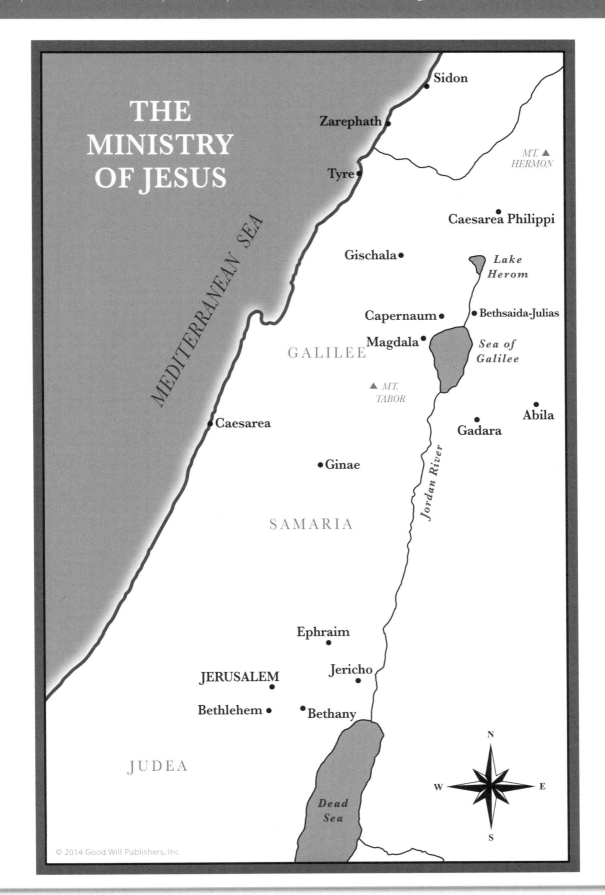

THE MINISTRY OF JESUS

MEDITERRANEAN SEA

Sidon

Zarephath

Tyre

MT. ▲ HERMON

Caesarea Philippi

Gischala•

Lake Herom

Capernaum• •Bethsaida-Julias

Magdala• *Sea of Galilee*

GALILEE

▲ *MT. TABOR*

Abila

Gadara•

•Caesarea

•Ginae

Jordan River

SAMARIA

Ephraim
•

Jericho
•

JERUSALEM
•

Bethlehem • •Bethany

JUDEA

Dead Sea

N
W   E
S

START

FINISH

Christ the Great Teacher Word Search Clues

1. Jesus talked about prayer: "When you are praying, don't multiply your words, as the _____ do."

2. In His Sermon on the Mount, Jesus gave us the eight _____.

3. Peter asked, "How often must I forgive my brother who sins against me? Seven times?" Jesus taught about _____, saying, "Not seven times, but seventy times seven times."

4. Jesus taught the eight beatitudes during His _____ on the Mount.

5. The _____ usually treated Samaritans with contempt.

6. Jesus told a story of a rich man and a poor man who lay at his gate named _____.

7. The gospel tells us often how Jesus would spend the whole night in _____.

8. In the story of the Good Samaritan, after the priest passed by the dying man, a _____ also passed him by.

9. "_____ the Lord your God with all your heart, and with all your soul, and with all your strength."

10. Jesus taught about the _____ and taught that the home is the place where we first learn how to love one another.

11. Jesus compared the things of God to things from everyday life. He spoke about them in _____.

12. Although the Jews treated these people with contempt, it was the _____ who helped the dying man after the priest and Levite had passed him.

Christ the Great Teacher Word Search

```
F D S N P Y E S Z S I G
T O V E L R E V A L B B
Z J R I L R A M O N E Y
G F M G M B A Y I L A Z
E A I O I R A L E P T U
F N N X I V Y R N R I S
I X Z T O P E W A O T U
O N A E H R E N T P U R
E N S E L I T N E G D A
L E V I T E O P G S E Z
S W E J S S V J Q U S A
G H G U Y T G M D Z C L
```

If you have trouble figuring out the words from your clues, see if you can find the words from this list: Beatitudes, Family, Forgiveness, Gentiles, Jews, Lazarus, Levite, Love, Parables, Prayer, Priest, Samaritan, Sermon

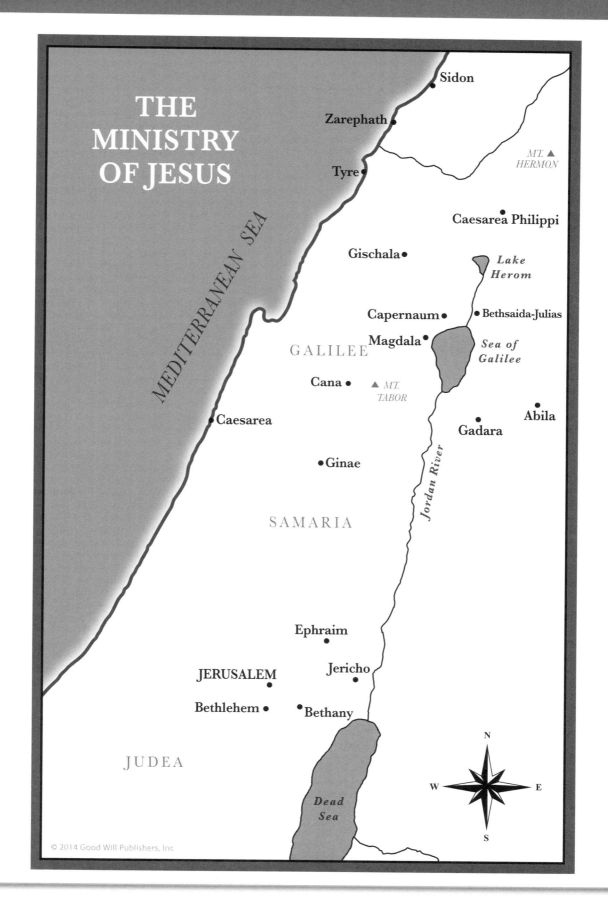

THE
MINISTRY
OF JESUS

MEDITERRANEAN SEA

Sidon

Zarephath

MT. ▲
HERMON

Tyre

Caesarea Philippi

Gischala

Lake
Herom

Capernaum   Bethsaida-Julias

GALILEE   Magdala

Sea of
Galilee

Cana   ▲ MT.
TABOR

Abila

Caesarea

Gadara

Jordan River

Ginae

SAMARIA

Ephraim

Jericho

JERUSALEM

Bethlehem   Bethany

JUDEA

N

W   E

S

Dead
Sea

Across

3. Where was the Sea in which Jesus walked on water and calmed the storm?
6. What did Jesus walk on that made His apostles think He was a ghost?
7. Where did Jesus tell His apostles to row across the Sea of Galilee to after calming the storm?
8. What did Jesus change the water into at the wedding feast?

Down

1. Who asked Jesus to perform His first miracle?
2. Where were Christ and His apostles traveling to when Jesus cursed the fig tree?
4. Who tried to walk on water to meet Jesus?
5. What did Jesus have to calm to put His apostles at ease?
7. Where did the wedding feast take place?

Christ and the Sick Word Search Clues

1. Bartimaeus said, "_____, let me receive my sight."
2. While staying in _____, Jesus healed many afflicted with various diseases and cast out many demons.
3. The people in Capernaum who were brought to Jesus were poor and _____.
4. Some of the most beautiful miracles Jesus performed were those of healing, showing Our Lord's great _____ for those who were afflicted.
5. The Roman centurion had great _____, because he believed Jesus could heal by just saying the word.
6. On the Sabbath, Jesus saw a blind man who was begging for _____.
7. Jesus showed great _____ by absolving the sick from not only illness of the body but of the soul as well.
8. The _____ would throw away their crutches. The blind open their eyes and see for the first time.
9. _____ were often forced to live outdoors, on the rocky hillsides or in the desert.
10. Some of the most beautiful _____ that Jesus performed were those of healing.
11. Someone unable to see is _____.
12. They lowered the _____ man on a stretcher through the roof.
13. The _____ were outraged, thinking Jesus was committing blasphemy by saying He could forgive sins.
14. Those who are the opposite of rich.
15. What were the people called who followed Jesus and taught in His name?
16. They lowered the paralyzed man through the _____ so that Jesus could heal him.
17. The Pharisees were outraged that Jesus was healing people on the _____, a day meant for rest.
18. One woman who lived in Capernaum was healed just by touching Jesus' _____.
19. The woman who touched Jesus' clothes was immediately healed of her _____.
20. Jesus told the paralyzed man, "Son, your _____ are forgiven."

Christ and the Sick Word Search

```
S  S  E  N  E  V  I  G  R  O  F  B
U  F  O  O  R  S  D  G  S  M  L  A
F  V  I  I  S  N  I  S  N  I  K  B
F  M  A  S  H  I  S  J  N  R  P  C
E  S  U  S  R  T  C  D  E  A  T  L
R  A  L  A  M  E  I  K  R  C  A  O
I  B  J  P  N  P  P  A  N  L  G  T
N  B  P  M  O  R  L  E  F  E  O  H
G  A  A  O  W  Y  E  M  L  S  S  E
C  T  R  C  Z  X  S  P  A  W  V  S
M  H  S  E  E  S  I  R  A  H  P  D
Y  I  D  I  B  B  A  R  F  C  W  O
```

If you have trouble figuring out the words from your clues, see if you can find the words from this list: Alms, Blind, Capernaum, Clothes, Compassion, Disciples, Faith, Forgiveness, Lame, Lepers, Miracles, Paralyzed, Pharisees, Poor, Rabbi, Roof, Sabbath, Sickness, Sins, Suffering.

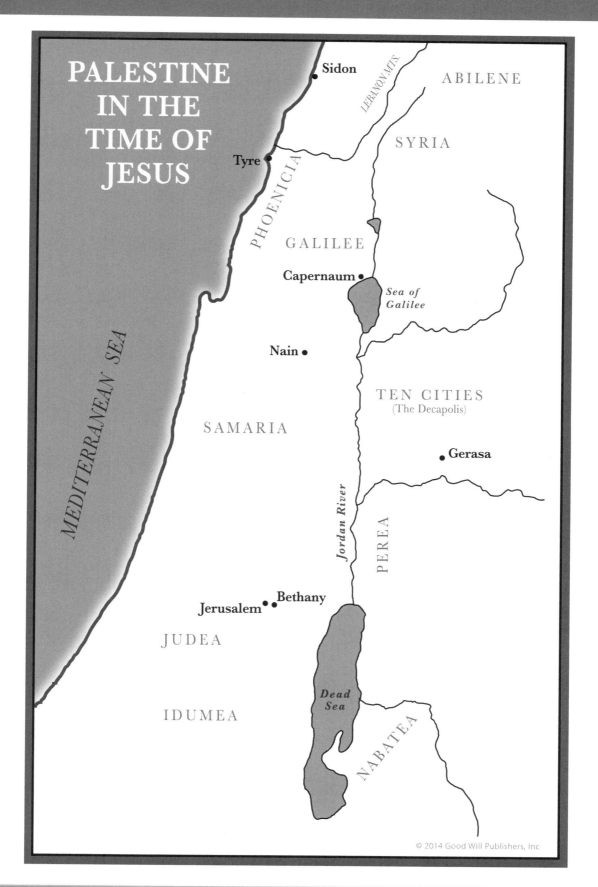

PALESTINE IN THE TIME OF JESUS

Across

2. Jesus told His disciples they would see Him coming in the _____ of heaven with great power and majesty.
7. Jesus told the rich young man he must sell all his things, and give the money to the _____.
8. What trade did Jesus work as a young man?
9. We can see that Jesus was poor from the beginning as He was born in a _____.

Down

1. Jesus' description of the Great _____ emphasizes the importance of charity.
3. Whose gift of two copper coins was greater than those who gave large sums?
4. Jesus said those with _____ had a hard time entering the Kingdom of Heaven.
5. Jesus said, "Blessed are the poor in _____ for theirs is the kingdom of heaven."
6. Jesus and His disciples depended on _____ from the people for their bodily needs.

Across

1. They sold the doves, pigeons, and other animals for sacrifice in the Temple.
5. Jesus made this to drive the merchants and moneychangers out of the Temple.
7. These people love to stand and pray in the synagogues and on the street corners to be seen by others.
9. A pool in Jerusalem.
10. The day the Law of Moses commanded the Jews to keep holy.
12. Jesus saw the merchants and moneychangers as He passed through the Court of the _____.
13. The place Jesus spent His youth.

Down

2. He was an enemy of Jesus and hated Him because he was afraid of Him and thought Jesus was John the Baptist returned from the dead.
3. He was a member of the Sanhedrin who was a secret disciple of Jesus.
4. They gave the people Jewish money in exchange for Roman money in the Temple.
6. These enemies of Jesus lived hypocritical lives and had little true love of God.
8. A book written on a long scroll of specially prepared sheep or goatskin. This was called _____.
11. Jesus told a parable of the great _____ to teach about the kingdom of heaven.

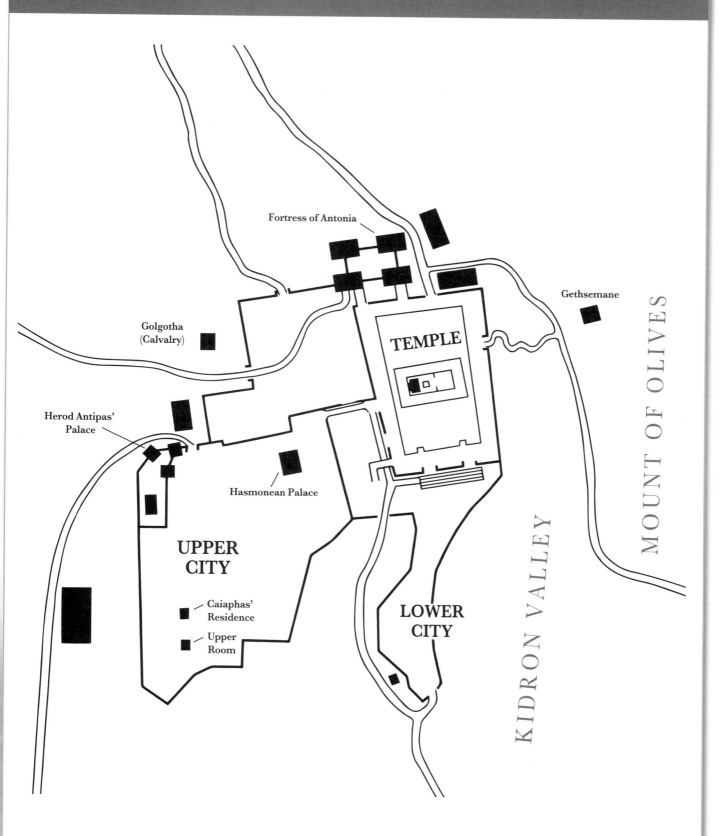

Fortress of Antonia

Gethsemane

TEMPLE

Golgotha
(Calvary)

MOUNT OF OLIVES

Herod Antipas'
Palace

Hasmonean Palace

UPPER
CITY

Caiaphas'
Residence

Upper
Room

LOWER
CITY

KIDRON VALLEY

Christ is Crucified Word Search Clues

1. Jesus refused the wine mixed with _____ that they offered Him.
2. "And for My clothing they cast _____."
3. Who wrote the title for Jesus' cross reading, "Jesus of Nazareth, King of the Jews"? _____
4. He was the high priest at the time of Christ's crucifixion. _____
5. A _____ rode at the head of the procession to Calvary.
6. Jesus' _____ was at the foot of the cross, and took John as her son that day.
7. The soldiers divided Our Lord's outer _____, belt, and sandals.
8. Jesus' body was placed in a _____.
9. Jesus was crucified on a _____.
10. The Roman way of putting criminals to death. _____
11. The father-in-law of Caiaphas, the high priest. _____
12. The friends of Jesus had _____ Him.
13. "They divide My _____ among them."
14. He was from Cyrene and helped carry the cross. _____
15. This name means "place of the skull." _____
16. Died on the cross to save us from our sins. _____
17. The procession to Calvary began at the _____.
18. They drove _____ into His hands and feet.
19. Two _____ were crucified on His left and right.
20. The crucifixion took place on the hill known as _____ .

Christ Is Crucified Word Search

```
M  N  P  S  C  L  K  S  A  N  N  A
V  O  R  A  H  T  O  G  L  O  G  F
P  M  A  H  E  T  Q  T  I  I  O  E
Q  I  E  P  T  Q  F  X  S  R  A  O
Y  S  T  A  A  X  I  E  S  U  T  P
R  I  O  I  L  F  K  A  T  T  B  E
A  M  R  A  I  I  K  H  N  N  I  T
V  Y  I  C  P  E  I  B  E  E  J  C
L  R  U  S  N  E  T  E  M  C  L  N
A  R  M  G  V  S  S  C  R  O  S  S
C  H  R  E  H  T  O  M  A  X  T  O
J  E  S  U  S  S  I  K  G  L  T  C
```

If you have trouble figuring out the words from your clues, see if you can find the words from this list: Annas, Caiaphas, Calvary, Centurion, Cloak, Cross, Crucifixion, Forsaken, Garments, Golgotha, Jesus, Lots, Mother, Myrrh, Pilate, Praetorium, Simon, Spikes, Thieves, Tomb

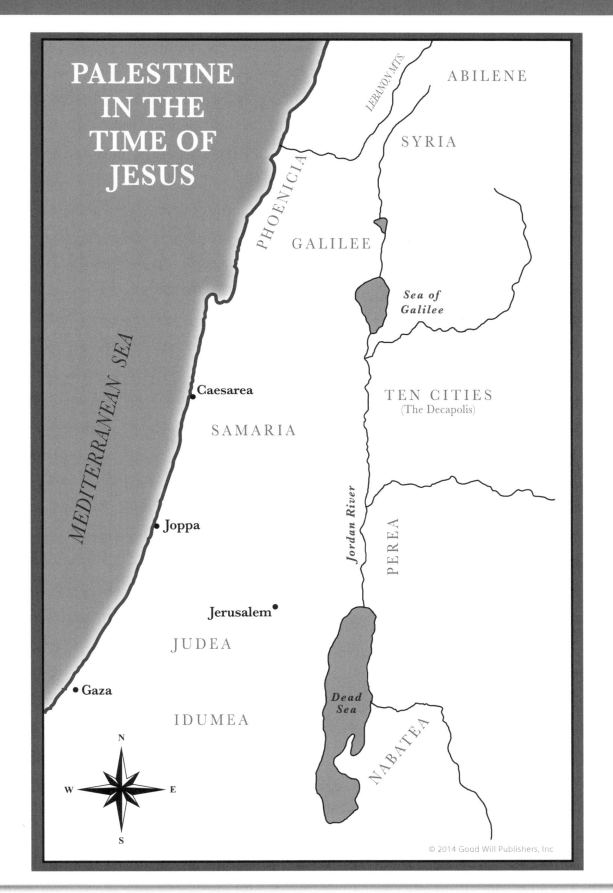

PALESTINE
IN THE
TIME OF
JESUS

ABILENE

SYRIA

LEBANON MTS.

PHOENICIA

GALILEE

*Sea of
Galilee*

MEDITERRANEAN SEA

• Caesarea

SAMARIA

TEN CITIES
(The Decapolis)

Jordan River

• Joppa

PEREA

Jerusalem •

JUDEA

• Gaza

*Dead
Sea*

IDUMEA

NABATEA

N
W   E
S

© 2014 Good Will Publishers, Inc

Seed of God Word Search Clues

1. A great city in Syria. _____
2. The region where Cornelius, the Roman centurion lived. _____
3. A Roman centurion who believed in the one true God. _____
4. The _____ man who spoke to Philip in his chariot.
5. The king who lived in Jerusalem and persecuted the Church. _____
6. The city where Tabitha lived. _____
7. The region where Christianity began; Jerusalem is located here. _____
8. The city where a paralyzed man named Aeneas resided. _____
9. The apostle who led the Church. _____
10. A deacon who went to Samaria to preach and work miracles. _____
11. The land of Samaritans. _____
12. A young man who watched the stoning of Stephen and approved. _____
13. A deacon who was stoned to death for his faith. _____
14. A disciple of Jesus who was known for devoting herself to good works and acts of charity; Peter raised her from the dead. _____

Seed of God Word Search

```
E  G  K  O  S  G  P  S  J  I  P  L
C  T  F  S  X  G  S  N  Q  Z  G  I
A  J  H  A  I  R  A  M  A  S  H  C
E  U  Y  I  F  X  N  B  Z  O  E  N
S  D  N  C  O  R  N  E  L  I  U  S
A  E  L  E  V  P  A  L  P  H  L  A
R  A  J  O  H  N  I  I  U  Y  L  H
E  W  O  O  T  P  L  A  D  A  W  T
A  K  K  I  P  I  E  I  N  U  S  I
V  X  O  G  H  P  A  T  T  Y  W  B
T  C  F  P  R  K  A  Y  S  I  N  A
H  E  R  O  D  R  E  T  E  P  N  T
```

If you have trouble figuring out the words from your clues, see if you can find the words from this list: Antioch, Caesarea, Cornelius, Ethiopian, Herod, Joppa, Judea, Lydia, Peter, Philip, Samaria, Saul, Stephen, Tabitha

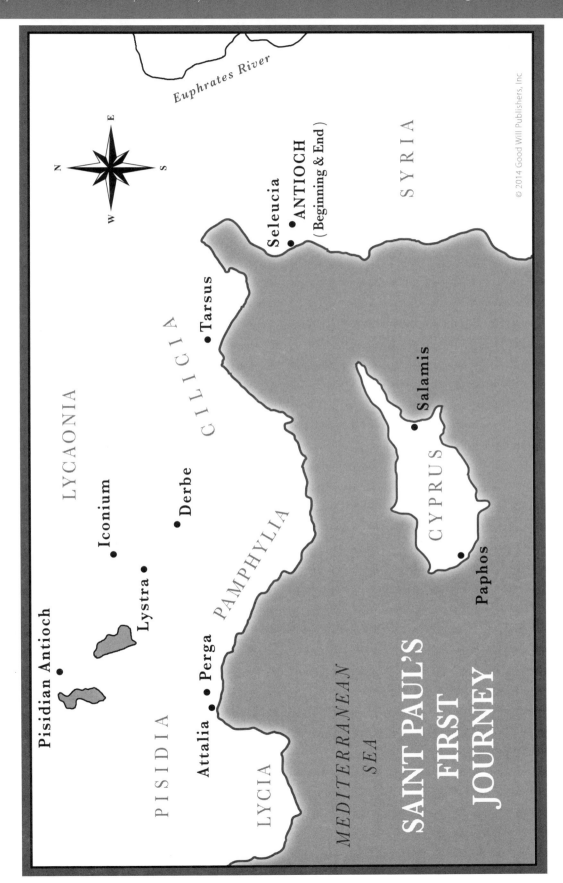

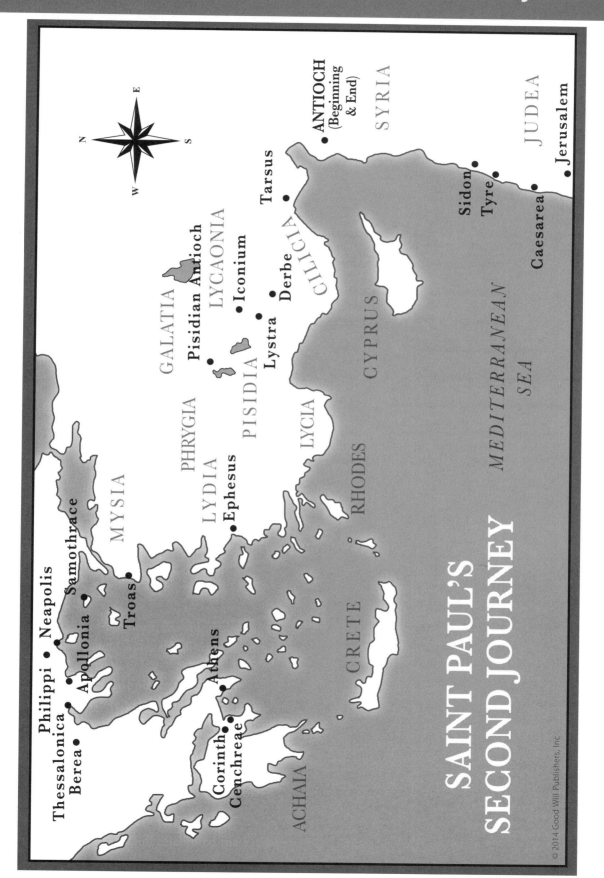

SAINT PAUL'S SECOND JOURNEY

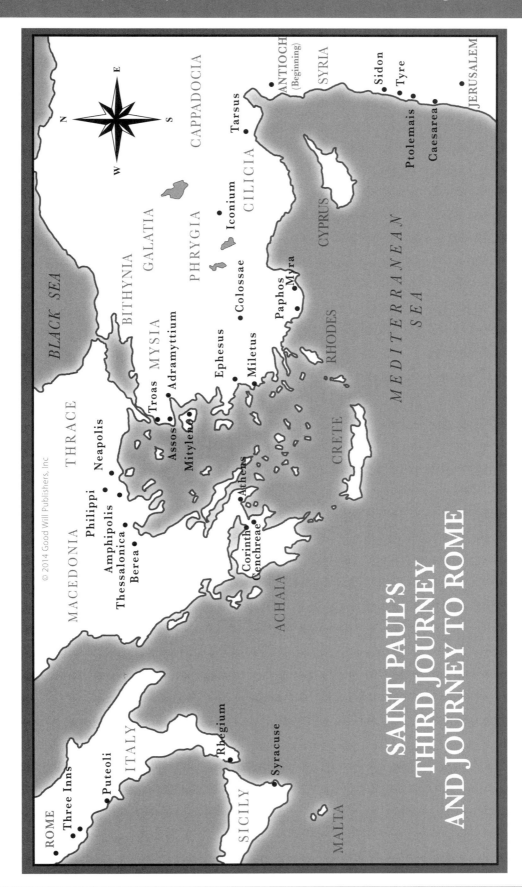

SAINT PAUL'S
THIRD JOURNEY
AND JOURNEY TO ROME

© 2014 Good Will Publishers, Inc

Across

2. Greek goddess of the hunt, worshiped by pagans.
4. Paul was convinced God wanted him to return here.
5. The feast of the Holy Spirit.
7. A silversmith who felt threatened by Paul's teaching because his trade depended on the worship of the false god.
9. People who worshiped false gods.
11. A place not far from Ephesus where Paul gave a farewell address.
12. The young man who fell out of window.
13. A city Paul traveled to and celebrated the Eucharist in an upper room.

Down

1. A great city where believers only knew of the baptism of John.
3. These people made silver shrines of Artemis and sold them for a living.
6. People spoke in _____ and prophesied when the Holy Spirit came on them.
8. Objects that were worshiped by pagans.
10. Paul departed from _____ and set out on his third missionary journey.

FINISH

START

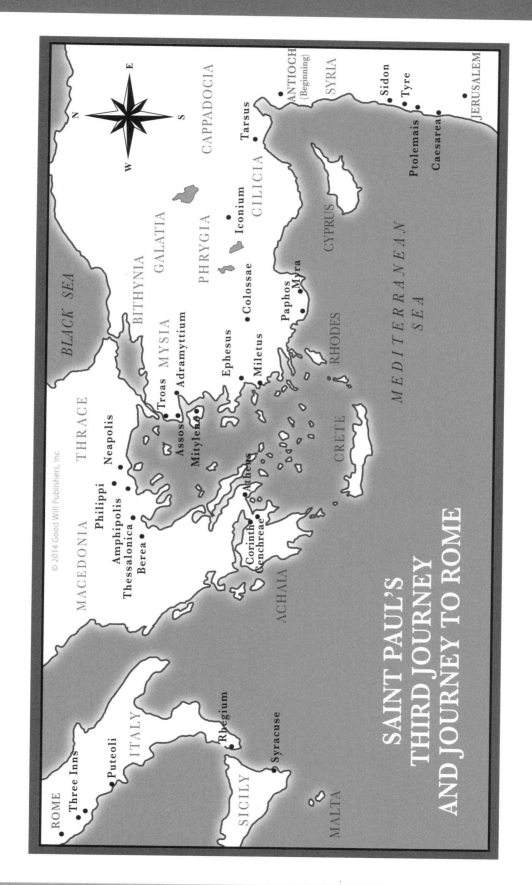

SAINT PAUL'S
THIRD JOURNEY
AND JOURNEY TO ROME

© 2014 Good Will Publishers, Inc

Acknowledgments

Creating the Activity Book for *The Story of the Bible* was a large project, made possible by many talented and generous people.

Thank you to the many moms, teachers, church groups, and others who generously shared their ideas and creativity, in person and online. For Story of the Bible, I drew inspiration in particular from: www.mowcopchurch.com, www.catholicinspired.com, catholicplayground.com, and www.mssscrafts.com. The puzzle generators at discoveryeducation.com, crosswordlabs.com, and mazegenerator.net were valued resources as well.

I thank the Saint Benedict Press team for all of their hard work and dedication in making this project come together, including: Mara Persic, art director; Caroline Kiser, graphic designer; Nick Vari, production editor; and Morgan Witt, editorial intern.

Lastly, I would like to thank my family for all their love and support. My children, Aiden, Mary, Patrick, Peter, Jude, Paul, Teresa, Imelda, David and Annie are a daily source of inspiration for me. Without them this book would not exist. And Conor Gallagher, my publisher, is also my husband. I love you, Conor, and am blessed beyond measure to have you as both.

TAN·BOOKS

TAN Books was founded in 1967 to preserve the spiritual, intellectual and liturgical traditions of the Catholic Church. At a critical moment in history TAN kept alive the great classics of the Faith and drew many to the Church. In 2008 TAN was acquired by Saint Benedict Press. Today TAN continues its mission to a new generation of readers.

From its earliest days TAN has published a range of booklets that teach and defend the Faith. Through partnerships with organizations, apostolates, and mission-minded individuals, well over 10 million TAN booklets have been distributed.

More recently, TAN has expanded its publishing with the launch of Catholic calendars and daily planners—as well as Bibles, fiction, and multimedia products through its sister imprints Catholic Courses (CatholicCourses.com) and Saint Benedict Press (SaintBenedictPress.com). In 2015, TAN Homeschool became the latest addition to the TAN family, preserving the Faith for the next generation of Catholics (www.TANHomeschool.com).

Today TAN publishes over 500 titles in the areas of theology, prayer, devotions, doctrine, Church history, and the lives of the saints. TAN books are published in multiple languages and found throughout the world in schools, parishes, bookstores and homes.

For a free catalog, visit us online at
TANBooks.com

Or call us toll-free at
(800) 437-5876